# LITTLE-KNOWN OPERAS

Also by Patrick Donnelly

*Jesus Said*
*Nocturnes of the Brothel of Ruin*
*The Charge*

Translations with Stephen D. Miller

*The Wind from Vulture Peak: The Buddhification of Japanese* Waka *in the Heian Period*

# LITTLE-KNOWN OPERAS

Patrick Donnelly

Four Way Books
Tribeca

Library of Congress Cataloging-in-Publication Data
Names: Donnelly, Patrick, 1956- author.
Title: Little-known operas / Patrick Donnelly.
Description: New York, NY : Four Way Books, 2019. |
Includes bibliographical references.
Identifiers: LCCN 2018028724 | ISBN 9781945588310 (pbk. : alk. paper)
Classification: LCC PS3604.O5634 A6 2019 | DDC 811/.6--dc23
LC record available at https://lccn.loc.gov/2018028724
This book is manufactured in the United States of America and printed on acid-free paper.

Four Way Books is a not-for-profit literary press. We are grateful for the assistance we receive from individual donors, public arts agencies, and private foundations.

This publication is made possible with public funds from the New York State Council on the Arts, a state agency.

We are a proud member of the Community of Literary Magazines and Presses

Contents

For Diane Seuss,

dear virtuoso

## A postcard of *Christ Carrying the Cross*,

circle of Giovanni Bellini circa 1505 oil on wood, is what
he fits between his third and fourth weekly pill boxes,

to remind himself to reorder. His routine about the anti-
virals is of greater magnitude, maybe, than the one in which

Mrs. Gardner used to place a vase of violets in front
of the painting, when she owned it. This card's only

a reproduction of the Passion, not the original. But we've seen
how imitation and daily use can make of pity and fear

an almost cozy utensil. The Savior's torso is pointed
toward the royal climb, but his unreadable eye turns out,

loosing on you, passerby, a tear of blood and milk.

## Which makes me, I guess, the muddy Colorado

. . . Carved with the curious legend of my youth . . .
—Stanley Kunitz

What we learn from most pornography is
that a great many primates so professionally beautiful
as to make one's teeth ache
have had congress with a great many other such primates,
though only a few seemed really that into it.

What only a specialized, expensive, or amateur category of porn
reveals is that occasionally one of the immortals will,
as in Cavafy's poem, condescend to love up
an ordinary person. Even the Grand Canyon
was full before it was empty: over the eons

many breathtaking, sometimes medicated concavities
have been filled to overspilling by unexceptional convexities
who just happened to lean into the right gloaming, urinous doorway
at a lucky small hour of the night. Even I,
who about 1981 heard a boy I loved at summer camp in Maine

tell a girl, when he thought I was asleep, that he might have loved me
*except that I was not good looking*—I, even *I*, in time
came to have such regular traffic with gods lovelier than he

as to shake my teeth all but loose. Was this because
I got better looking, or just that even the gods' hungers

have their reasons *que la raison ne connaît pas*? Whatever.
This fluid exchange lasted so many years that
even what was often over-praised as "hard as rock"
wore down by degrees to the steep ditch you see
before you. (I began tall but was brought both low and deep.)

Though I don't recommend
the vulgar glass overlook, still, *camerado*,
if you step to the edge of this
strange history, I promise you'll thrill
to the vast, acrophobic layers of emptiness—

# The chicken

Touching your goodness, I am like a man
who eats songbirds drowned in Armagnac
and roasted on a spit, as they've done
in France since Roman times. And you might think
he covers his head with a napkin so God won't see
and judge his shameful appetites. Truth is, he also knows
by heart the old Persian story, the holy fool Nasruddin
and other disciples told by their sheikh to go
and kill a chicken where no one could see. He remembers
only Nasruddin could find after many hours
no lonely place where he could not be seen—by the One,
not to mention the chicken. Watched, unwatched:
what would you call his feeling for the paradox
that keeps him seen and unseen, and beloved and alone?

*after William Meredith*

# Honey

*tu che il zucchero porti in mezzo al core*
—Lorenzo Da Ponte, *Don Giovanni*

Funny, how often in a long marriage the word *honey*
gets shouted as warning, for instance this morning

when he asked to keep a piss bottle by the side of the bed.

When he called for a ride because he was drunk,
when he mislaid the gift you gave.

How often *honey* as rebuke, only sometimes in irony,

while you yourself behave, you think,
like those who ladle soup for the poor.

When he blacked out with a kidney stone

and had to be lifted, had to be helped
to bathe for a month,
you lowering him

like a fireman, even the water

you poured hurting his white skin,
even the soap.

Gold the bees struggled to gather and guard,

which while you were courting
from under your Brooklyn balcony

he swore in a little age-of-enlightenment song

your mouth was sweeter than.
(His white shirt as he mounted

the steps, white shirt

soon on the floor.)
When he didn't make enough money, when

you had to carry him. Oh, wait,

the other faults—venial—were his, but it was *you*
who made no money, your deadweight

over his shoulders for years

while you wrote what you wrote. Yet still
you bark at him the name of the bee's treasure,

bellow *honey*, sometimes smothering, almost shaming

his mouth's sweet air, which swore
that first, famous night how

you "carry sugar in the middle of your heart."

# Jesus said to me Did you mean

to draw some moral
from your own life, how you found love

so late? How though you weren't patient,
weren't kind, in pursuit were ruthless,

it was given to you anyway? Though
that story's not done, not proven,

you have some wisdom to share
with the loveless now,

do you,
something they should or shouldn't do?

The gay boy, the raped girl, the libeled widow
(Jesus now resting his abraded hand on the book)?

Go ahead then, speak.
Promise them something.

## Jesus said Will someone

tell me, please, what this
pink grass is called? I see it
in a field east of 116 as I'm driving south,

also behind an old cemetery in Deerfield,
and in other waste places.

It hovers about seven inches,
rosy (color of wisdom) in late summer, then
when, in fall, dew or frost sends sparks

running in and out, it's like unto
gold tried in the furnace.

Jesus said, I may have said this before, but
consider the grass. How famous it is
for what it is. Nutritious. Useful, twisted

into ropes, woven as cloth or burned
as smudge over your

sometimes sick body.
So many characters the grass seems to be,
getting up from the fields

in the morning, companions
of the dew.

(*Fleeing the deep grasses of the hunting ground,*
Sokaku wrote, *I heard the stag cry*
*—my friend is lost—*)

Switch grass, blue grass, crab
grass, knot, quaking, *Leaves of*:

You used to go into the juice shop on 23rd Street
and you drank that wheatgrass as though
it could save you from the cry of a lonesome retrovirus.

And you did live, till now, lived to write that.
So many stories, as many as all beings. That's how many

fall in front of the mower,
companions of the fire, come evening.

## Jesus said There's a story

that I cursed a fig tree, *Ficus carica.*
I will say I understand people who hate

how loosely rooted are the petals of the peony,
*Paeonia lactiflora, Paeonia suffructicosa,* in its brackets.

One morning you cut the stem and carry it wet
from the garden, thinking "the lightest possible pink"
(and also, you being you, trying *not* to think "flecks of red,
menstrual, tubercular, Keats's
handkerchief"). Next afternoon

you notice the petals have gone
slightly crepey, more than one
brown or spotted.

The third day you'll be on your knees
sweeping up the shattered head.

In the news report about opposition to a local hospice
the NIMBY lady asked, "How can I be happy,
while that's across the street?"

An excellent question, *Homo erectus, Homo sapiens, Homo curiosum*. Another is,

on the cheek, on the chest,
on her shoulder or in his lymph, what role
can a brown spot, a purple spot, play
in delight?
                No, really,
what? Answer me.

# Jesus said A program

remembers, doesn't it, where you
stopped watching the movie,

where you clicked off those books
before shutting off the light.

Other programs remember
your searches, your queue, passwords, complaints,

the wallpaper you chose, how loud, how bright
you preferred things to be, your presence

in the streaming firmament.
What I want to know is,

after you've climbed up the seven-storey bardos
(louder and brighter than you prefer, I've heard),

how long do you think they'll remember your place,
hold it open for you, keep it warm?

# Blood moon

Came a red moon the night between the Easter vigil
and the morning of the resurrection and that shade

made a horizontal of the window rail and a vertical

of half the curtain, *a cross*—and because I wasn't well
(some spring distemper) lying alone in the guest room

where we also kept a small shrine and our mothers' ashes

Stephen sleeping on an upper floor but I wasn't asleep
the moon too bright and part of me knowing I had begun

to see a cross only because it was almost Easter 2015

and another part said *but I'm not the* kind *of person who sees*
*crosses in curtains* long finished with The Church or churches

but nevertheless here at first seemed to be *three* shadows

three crosses just like in the story which after a time became
one and then O shit a tree The Tree the World Tree the tree

of the world and behind my eyes came a kind of light

and I thought to myself I have not recently taken drugs
have I or gone strictly-speaking crazy like Philip K. Dick

who experienced his *Vast Active Living Intelligence System*

as a pink illumination bearing the message that his infant son
had some kind of knot in his gut that could kill him (which

a reluctant doctor confirmed and saved him from)

and have I anyway gotten my antidepressant dosage right?
My light too though not pink was somewhat real because

after a while it went away which is the test of real things

and then it was night again *noche oscura* as St. John of the Cross
might have put it and I knew I was in danger of making of all this

*a meaning* because it was Easter and outside the rabbits

fucked in the chamomile wearing burdock burrs like crowns
but still could there have been any part which was not just

of my making Christ the vertical and the horizontal Christ

Ygdrassil the Allfather hanging nine days without food or drink
Christ the plane tree *Platanus orientalis* with lights in it

that Xerxes stopped his armies to adore and away from which

he would not move again until his goldsmith struck the image
on a medal which afterwards he wore always next to his heart.

At 11:11 in the morning from this vision I awoke I who do not

have visions or want any but for all that is the sad world not yet
utterly emptied of parable? Does the young corn still put

his ear above the soil like a flute?

—April 4, 2015, Blood Moon

# Throne Verse

Two years of cinders built up in the hearth,
the new over and over the old.

I'd made nothing for months, just consumed
or operated what others made.

Pointless to say what, but I will: frozen food,
my name on petitions to save various things,

a spray for scale on the plants,
films that streamed to me from a link,

sometimes viewed from our bed, which
either went unmade or was made so particularly

as the only task I could complete all day
that I would not let my love help

and accused him
of not knowing how.

Before this, I'd made an effort, sent it out
for judgment and could make nothing else till I heard.

But did I have to compare every breath I drew
to "an angioplasty"?

Did I have to be so sad?
Did I have to be as sad as my mother had been sad

and in the same way,
and hadn't I lectured her before she went

not to make her sadness a burden for others,
and by others hadn't I meant me?

A job of work was what had vexed me,
three years, or eight years, or fifty-four, depending.

The time might have wished to release to me
some money or some other boon,

but not right there or then,
the hour wasn't right. So those things collected upriver

behind some kind of dam,
like jellies in a larder, jars of garnets I couldn't lift from the water,

garnets from Kenya, Finland, Rajasthan, the Ural Mountains,
pomegranates, gooseberries, stones made of cinnamon, live coals.

Are you the type of person who doesn't need approval?

Who keeps on working, no matter what?
Like God, whose throne, it is written, extends

over the heavens and the earth
and who "feels no fatigue in guarding and preserving them"?

Well, good for you—right now I don't care to lift
even the thinnest, netherest edge of the counterpane.

Nobody has yet said
we can't afford to hold up the whole Internet forever,

but that's right, don't you see? We'll have to vote
which parts to lose, which secret giant facilities

to keep cool with electricity made from burning coals.
Will it be the levels of games, the libraries, or the paths to the lonesome

no-talking-no-kissing-no-reciprocating hook-ups?
That was the link from which I somehow met my love,

and now it's all gone—click there, if you don't believe.
Even the gate has disappeared, from when

America was Online. Now the young flood
along other routes, open to them alone.

Wasn't it two months before the crazy old girl died
that I wrote in a letter I must have sent

TO HER HOSPITAL BED, for Christ's sake,
that "the kindest thing anyone could do for others

is to face their own fears"? And didn't she reply
she was "not up to being challenged on any part

of her worldview right then"? Whatever happened
to her garnet wedding band? Sweet bloody prophets and saints,

at least I turned off the screens to write this,
several days running, at least I worked.

Just how long might you be inclined
to help me lift my heavy head

off its throne of heaped and burning dung?

## Standing and moving

My God, through the night's susceptible hours I search
with my tongue for some formula for remembering You,
one that doesn't insist on Your Oneness, which I doubt.
*There is no God but God* tastes funny to me, bad funny,
because though, okay, as Rukeyser said about islands,
*O for God's sake, / they are connected / underneath,*
above the surface You are many gods, a hard rain of gods in fact.
You are the Dry River, the Black Brook, Lost Lake, Small Hidden Falls
and the sweet water of Maryland's Prettyboy Reservoir.
You are the subfusc Hour of the Rat, and Myōken the pole star.
You are a current forcing Yourself North, wind resisting
Your progress, tides rushing up and down the channel,
confused and dangerous. You are table mountains, arches, and domes,
standing stones in an oval, Long Meg and Her Daughters.
And how can You not be the terrible ancient cedars at Okunoin,
the mossy graves and hollow underplaces of Dis, Tartarus, and Yomi,
realms of white moths and trippy organ pipes,
as well as foxes, words, ghosts, honey, oils, and noises?
In the past You've hid in the mystery of swords, mirrors,
and comma-shaped jewels. More recently
the god Hermes showed himself
to my friend Diane as Freddie Mercury at about age 39,
and I know a guy who leaves a five-yen coin
on the windowsill as an offering to whatever the view is that day.

To me You've appeared as certain verbs such as *beheld*
in English or *blanchir* in French, in the music, the drumming,
if not the argument of *la ilaha illalllah*, and in some gestures,
such as the half-moon night in 1987 when a pale
god named Bruno leaned over to kiss oh thirsty me, young and
transfigured on the dance floor at the Parliament House in Orlando,
the memory of which is bodies of water, both standing and moving.

# Five objections to the practice of hammering nails into the heels of a corpse

One—into her *heels*, my mother's poor heels
already rough and swelled and chapped?
So she wouldn't "walk abroad," unquiet?
*This* your best angle?
Two, it's ignorant.
You're ignorant.
Three, there must be other ways
of appeasing, averting . . .
certain herbs, basil, nettle, picked
at midnight, bruised in front
of her photograph? Or
what if I copy
some of her favorite lines
over and over with gold ink,
make a sutra of them, my nib
whispering memorial over the parchment,
*the moss is grown, the different mosses, /*
*Too deep to clear them away!* If there are gods and if
gods want poems and are fed and consoled
by poems, might not—her restless . . .
Four, you didn't know her. Today
she'd have a diagnosis and some pills to take.

But if she, as she was, wished to walk
    on her dead heels,
if she chose to reveal herself to my nephew
    riding happy with the band The White Stripes
in a limo till the driver lowered the glass
    that separated the front from the back and *she*
was the driver, her mouth a bald socket
    about to speak in the rearview mirror—
if she insisted on appearing
    as a particularly shiny crow
hammering her bonebeak at my window
    on the anniversary—no,
no nail could stop her. No hammer,
    no stake in the world.

(Five: hammering at her reflection,
    is what I guess,
her own hated image.)
    Bonebeak, crowsocket, nailnib.

## Written on the mirror in steam,

Jesus's note read—

Try to remember who I was
before you heard my name—

# Jesus asked,

When one looks
at Japanese
scroll paintings

of waterfalls—
*taki*, black ink
on white silk,

those unfurlings
of negative space
suggesting mist

and falling water,
supposedly
so cooling

in summer—
how conceivably
to avoid thinking

the word
"pubic"?
Those jutting rocks, those

overhanging tufts
of grasses,
humid and peaty? A poet

wrote *Pictures*
*are hard*
*to see . . . And people*

*are hard to love*, but it's
harder still
to unsee how

sex is every solitary thing's
verge—cresting sweet mess of wet
before falling—

# Jesus said You will not

be able to catch
the swan boat
                    of your youth
by running after it like that.

I know it was pretty,
I know it didn't linger,
I know the pier caught fire

and sank.
            *Wait,* he said. *Tarry a while*
*alongside the wreck.* I don't say this
to everyone: but there will come

another swan.

# Jesus said, "Buddhas of limitless light,"

a phrase encountered by accident, let's say,
on an old scroll or overheard. Afterward,

would it be impossible to feel so doubting and blue
about people? Never again so stagy, so *show-me*,

so heart-hurt—even if there are no
Buddhas of limitless light?

## Some temples

The blood ceiling,
which used to be the blood floor.

Ranks of glimmering, choiring
in praise of shadows.

The guidebook says there was
a famous duel on the porch.

A garden fountain that cures crying.
Maybe yours, maybe ours, maybe only that of babies.

Ceiling of frog crotches.
I went through twice, the mercies leaning

not, for once, away.
Thunder struck his eight drums.

Strength, stripped to the waist, shoved down
one palm, punched one fist out

from his shoulder, right, left.
One offered her hand, apron of eyes.

One made solemn.
One the peacock avatar of a general.

One ate incense.
One's hair was on fire, of course.

One made rain,
scepter and tiara of tree snakes.

Two women passed right to left
before the mercies, violin cases

over their shoulders. A handsome
young man, handsome feet bare.

Was I ever that bare?
Over the huge mother of mercies the hung bells.

Around her the fierce courante of kings, torquing, running.
Headdress of lady fingers.

One listened who struck the cymbals.
One smiled with teeth.

Her old virgin eyes and hands pray for you.
His pennant raised.

Three faces, six arms.
His petal pectoral.

His gilded bird, his contraposto, his mirror.
Pointed goatee, animal skin, epaulettes of skulls, his guitar.

The one with a beak played the flute,
kept time with his foot.

One shouldered a dragon as Jesus
did his lamb.

Is there some place, I asked, where you can see
all the mercies at the same time?

His lunge, his glare, his bag of wind.
A few mercies missing for repairs.

Willows along the Shirakawa.
*Her salt tears fell from her, and soften'd the stones;*

*Sing willow willow willow*
How many lenses opening and closing

have pulled on the view
from Kiyomizu?

The weeping
cherries have finished

weeping. The screens
of pines, stones, mist, water.

American boy pouts
*boring, boring, boring.*

A carnival outside, meat on sticks.
Big black carp annoyed

with falling petals, which aren't
food. Women cooed

to the baby
blossoms.

The gutters full of petals.
In the back row I saw you, your glimmer.

## One day one flower

Glimpsed through an open door,
a simple summon,

hard to describe what was seen.
Then we lost the bar for a week, searched

many nights on the block where
it ought to have been. Kyoto, years ago.

When it appeared again, we said this is it.
Is it? Yes,

here
we are.

Chalkboard drawing of a goblet saying,
"Why not have some wine?"

Like Brigadoon turning up
only when it wishes to, or Frost's Grail,

"Under a spell so the wrong ones can't find it."
The master nodding as we entered.

We the third couple.
A man and a woman, two women, we two men,

every kind of couple. We foreign,
older, dry, thirsty, full of care.

No images, everything dim
except for where he stood lit like a proscenium.

Faint music, Couperin, Ravel?
Of another time. The bar a slab of *keyaki*,

zelkova wood with a wide grain,
neither polished to a high sheen nor rough.

Lavender-scented *oshibori* on a wooden tray.
No bottle in sight,

no glasses, no images, no idols. One flower
in a vase on the wall, later we'd learn

picked from the banks
of the Shirakawa. But I'm getting ahead. Tonight

retrieving what the man to the right ordered.
Vermouth measured and mixed with

a long spoon on a spiral shaft.
To what shall I liken the bowl of the spoon?

Silver petal, mouse's ear of beaten tin.
When you dine with the devil, bring a long spoon,

one of us said. *Is* he a devil? Handsome enough.
Hair shining like an otter, shaved on the sides,

long in back and pulled to a tail. Samurai, courtly,
another century. Lifting with tongs

from some hidden place, a single parallelepiped of ice.
Fog spilling off, shape adjusted with a little chisel,

soda poured, ice pushed gentle down to mix.
A drop emptied to the back of his hand,

from there tasted or breathed. A balance
weighed, judged, the glass translated across.

An actor, you said, the bar his stage.
Yes. No, a priest, the bar his altar.

As in Fellini when a Spaniard, face in shadow,
mixes sangria, offers the mass,

transforms the elements. What's to eat
is on a handwritten menu (silly): hot dog,

two kinds of potato salad, "pur-een." (Pudding.)
Returning from the *toire* upstairs—

I said, I think he lives upstairs.
Kitchen table, high chair for a baby.

Over the toilet, a book,
*One Day, One Flower.*

Moving as the blind beggar monk
in the torchlit Nō play, his reconciliation

with his cruel father at the temple.
Important as the temple, as the mountain,

when he poured into the cup
I recognized him.

Hermes, Miroku, Al-Khidr,
the hidden guide.

Tell him he's an artist, is all I said.
Not my intention, he told you,

just a neighborhood drinking establishment.
OK, ask him how late he stays open.

*Owaru made.* Until it's finished. Until it's done.
He didn't quote Luke 12:49,

*I am come to sende fyre on the erth:*
*and what is my dysyre but that it were all redy kyndled?*,

but might as well have done.
Drunk when we left.

Less dry, less wrung out, younger.
What just happened, we asked.

I don't know, we answered.
Maybe every Latin poem proved

comparing being drunk to what
God's love feels like going and coming.

Maybe every cup a sangréal,
saké poured, wine spilling.

Ueda-san, your bar, now seen, now hidden.
Like how the moon can be a skull

and a cup can be a lamp.

# In which I explain why I set the fire

Well it began with a microburst from the North when the moon
was hot and bright on the Twenty-Sixth of the Fifth Month.
The first obstacle that wind met was the top of a White Pine
in the Neighbor of the Right's yard, which it shoved aslant
the transformer with a flash, killing the a/c for three days
and spoiling the fish. The Other White Pine, its mate,
the one I think of as male, didn't break. But afterward every time
I walked to the mailbox I had to say "One Broken, One Whole,"
and lift my hands over my head, whether I liked it or not.

The same night, the Sycamore of the Hayfield of the Right,
the one to which we make offerings at the New Year,
let fall into its crotch a log tall as a man. This tree
already weirdly suckled a Young Mimosa
in a few cups of soil in a high vertical cleft,
which explains why the Sycamore is worthy,
and why, not caring that drivers would stare,
I used to clap my hands each time I passed!
But when the wind gave the Sycamore this *lingam*,

a Member taller than a man, it was disturbing and not irrelevant.
I tried to lift and lay the extra part *parallel* to the road,
but it was heavier than three rough men bound together
(mechanics, say, or gas jockeys with slashes of black lubricant on their cheeks),

and I could not. One of the tree crews, gangs of bravoes
that came from this state and Connecticut and Vermont
lifted the crown and shoulders of the Female White Pine off the wires,
cut her into thirty-inch rounds and trucked all but the sawdust away.
But because to a rude man they had No Visual Sense,

they left the bollard-log hung from the Sycamore.
Which the Farmer of the Right also did nothing to rectify.
Nor was this all. At the North Border of the Hayfield of the Left,
a Poplar Shaped Like a Champagne Flute fell
perpendicular to the road that splits the Two Hayfields.
Now, perpendicular is better than crooked—of course—
though this turned up a clump of root that could scrape
the paint off the Right Side of Your Car
as you drive toward our house. But this also was not all.

*The tree did not die* though prostrated forty-point-five feet
into the Hayfield of the Left, which then no longer formed
a neat rectangle as seen from the house. No longer perfect,
it hurt me. The Farmer of the Left did not come with a chainsaw
and cut the Champagne Flute flush to the tree line,
nor with a backhoe and a thick cable to right it.
No—after that he let the Flute lie recumbent and *mowed around it*,
for which there was . . . good Lord, no word.

    What would *you* have called it? How

    would you have *fixed* it, this dog mess,<br>
God mess, flung to the Six Directions?<br>
    I lived this way long as I could. I tried<br>
to breathe release, be tolerant, busy inside myself.<br>
    Now I don't apologize—<br>
*the only way to cauterize a wound is with fire.*<br>
    Oh it hurt me, but now it is better.

    Wipe your feet. Don't track the ash inside.

## Poem contradicting the previous poem

He says the owner of the hay field did nothing,
and it is true he waited almost a year.
But on the last day of April three men came with a truck,
a tractor, and a chain saw, cut the fallen tree,
pulled the brush into the woods, and left
only tire tracks on the new grass.
There was no fire. There was never any fire.

# Jesus said *God*

*without Concepts.*

I said but
what about metaphor, simile, analogy, coyotes
yipping at the moon in the water?

Jesus said *God without Concepts.*

I said Doctors without Borders,
Dismissal without Prejudice,
Bath Time without Tears.

Jesus said *The Rothko Chapel.* Said, *Song without Words.*

I said
oh please you just broke your own rule.

And, I said, instead of Rothko's empty black and purple voids,
how about *Vierzehnheiligen* in Bavaria? Those creamy ovals,
s-curves, rococo, stucco, volutes, shells, floating bows—
witty teasing elusive architecture even Robert Venturi liked—
look it up.

Jesus said *GOD WITHOUT—*

but it was late and I had already hung anyway up on him.

# Jesus said Don't

try to draw me into an argument
about whether fairies can be saved:

There are in fact dumb questions.

A student asked Shri Mahayogi
When will Maitreya come?

Mahayogi asked for pencil and paper,
wrote a One, then covered the rest of the page
with Zeroes. He studied the Zeroes, erased
a few, asked for the Very Large Number

to be passed back to the student.

*Long time*, he said. *Long lonely time. Don't wait.*

# I dreamed that Jesus bid me go

and rake the ashes on Mount Golgotha,
looking for the poems he lost there.

My dear, don't weep, he said.

One of them began "A bead like amber
hung from pine"—so you may, he said,
find my virtue glinting in the dust.

The rosin of my heart, he said.

My dear, he said, my litter of lost rosin.

## Jesus said Papa

I don't feel You.

I don't feel right. I hear
nothing
on the lines where You
usually call.
                    Unless quote You unquote
are the peripheral zigzag of ocular migraine,
scintillating scotoma, that has smote me since I was twelve.

Arcs white or colored,
fine interleaving bands and ribbons that force me
to lie prostrate with the shades drawn,
and when I was younger to pull away from all of them,
my only comfort to touch myself in the dark.
                                                            Unless
mental afflictions are themselves

enlightenment, then yes, Your
comfortless loyal voice, my subduer, abaser, dishonorer,
I hear it, while suck

I on sweet ice. If that's Your voice, You
call me, You find me, offer me to drink
from that cup, everywhere
I've ever tried to hide.

## Modes of transmission

airborne: his breath: his glance:

his handwriting: his nickname

for you: and others of his secret accounts:

tears (his tears, also, causing yours):

the wearing of his ring:

sharing food from his plate:

thin wafer of cacao, beloved of God:

from his hand, taking his hand:

his hat, his headscarf, full of:

his scent, and oh Christ from his lips: his

spittle, parable, his plain song—

# The moon

We coupled like rabbits, me with hundreds,
hundreds with me, hundreds with hundreds
in those orgies on narrow beds at the baths.
Some nights their faces from the 80s rise—

Ken Ketwig
Stephen Simmons
Ramon Castaneda
Doyle Hardin
Michael Donatelli
Robbie Mittle
Peter Vom Lehn
Christopher Morrissey
Terry Cook . . .

Did you know there's a rabbit, not a man,
in the moon? Battering with his pestle,
pounding the new rice in his mortar,
crushing, releasing the elixir of life.

# The ninth day of Av

*Pneumocystis* pneumonia, his second case in the early 90s.
His bones soaking the sheets, his coughing which brought
up nothing. But when he'd close his eyes in the hospital bed
particular faces of people he'd never met in his inner eye

did rise up. Specific and aggressive and lacking bodies,
they wanted his, Beth Israel just one station of struggle
in those days. He barred their way with Jesus' name,
though the Catholic chaplain had *refused* him Jesus

in the form of bread, because he would not confess first.
"Where there is serious sin . . . " the priest said, trailing off.
Instead, the Jewish chaplain visited on Tisha B'Av,
and they spoke of the destruction of the Temple. Every night

he forbid the faces at the threshold, saying you cannot
come in. There is no extra room. I am still here in this body.

## Lorca's lips

Clumsy, coarse of feature, it is said.
One leg shorter than the other.

Liar, about works he intended to compose,
which he said were almost finished.

Which he hadn't even begun (like me,
spiller of seed, waster of his little time).

In mirrored cafes and at piano keyboards
gossiper, debater, uncombed, untied.

Carnal clown, answering the door in underpants,
Luis Cernuda naked on the daybed, explaining

"We were doing tumbling exercises."
Mooch, living pampered off Papá,

until in '31 he put on his blue overalls,
making from nothing a theater of the people,

sensuous, narrative, a school for
weeping and laughing,

like passing a consecrated host
from one mouth to another and another forever.

Weeper, who, told he'd be shot that day,
asked the guard "Will I be damned?"

(Whose bones they've never yet found, digging
under the olives at Fuente Grande.)

Truant, mystical, timid, pompous, distracted, kind.
His delicate moles,

the mourning cap of his hair
descending always to a peak.

Oh Lorca, you restless, lazy *maricón*, get up
suddenly and press the lips

of your shallow grave to mine.

# Jesus said Just when I think

I've heard everything Callas recorded,
I stumble on something new.

This Saint-Saëns thing I almost didn't click on
because it was, you know, Saint-Saëns,

"who stormed out of *The Rite of Spring* 29 May 1913,
infuriated over the misuse of the bassoon . . . "

Anyhow, '61, Paris, Callas with her musical friend
Georges Prêtre. Too bad they couldn't

have married as well, they were good together.
It was three years after her voice

was supposedly gone
she gave to one listener an experience he described

on YouTube:
*working with my dad in the chip shop . . . radio*

*on in the background, this was played.*
*i couldn't recognize the singer but remember saying*

*dad, she has to be*
*one of the greatest in the world her voice*

*confused me but how often*
*do we get a chance to listen as if the first time . . .*

His first time so close to her last time.
You, writing this, Jesus said, tried to be a singer

when you were young: you weren't good enough.
But Callas opened a neural pathway

through which the representations run,
masques of light and shade.

Maybe her voice had almost to be gone
before it could prove with inevitable

little slidings from one note to its neighbor or wider,
Dalila to Samson, that her confidence was shot

but not her throat, still changing every note's color,
all that has dark sounds, roots thrusting

into the fertile loam known to all of us,
ignored by all of us, a power and not a behavior,

a struggle and not a concept, not even in the throat
but surging up from the soles of the feet.
Her feet,

before which lay paradise.

## Maria Callas went to Hamburg

In 1959 when Maria Callas went to Hamburg her hair
was still neoclassical. In the film she emerges at 0 minutes:
7 seconds, silk legs the clapper of an underwater bell.

But the moment I need to tell about is at 42:30, prelude
of the *Pirata* aria, when resting her left hand
on the conductor's cage, head down eyes closed, cloistered,
thirty seconds forty fifty, she doesn't know us, we are nowhere and no one,
descending figure, strings distressed, dissonant, trembling, swelling,

(remember Mom in the '60s? her door closed sometimes till noon—)

## Crackup at 14:36

—the trouble starts at "woe to him" (Lady Macbeth, letter scene),
"who sets uncertain foot, and then retreats"—

—on "retreats" her mouth starts square, G, A, B, high CEEEEEE—

—then spreads, the C thins, curdles, acidic—

—but to me it's less important that she cracks
the high C—yes, she does, she did, 1959, moment 14:36—

—than what her face did, her hands—

—eyes widen/narrow/widen wider while she tries to save the note—

—after it splinters, all gone, went wrong so fast—

—her right hand apologizes—out from the breast, back, saying—

*—well, I tried—I practiced for 22 years, for instance—*

*—so for a moment,* (ten measures, horn, trumpet, trombone, strings)
*how about we shut our eyes and smile to ourselves—*

—then, side-eye to the conductor—*not your fault*—moving on:

"come on, hurry, I want to burn that cold heart of yours."

# YouTube: Broadcast Yourself

Go ahead, keep clicking around,
one of these days you'll find yourself

in the little swamp of blame
where people post the Black Pearls,

*Perle Nere,* fiasco, immortal voices cracking,
the singing kite plunging, tangling, bursting into flame,

drunk slurrings
and stumblings,

forgot where they were
or what they were supposed to do.

Room after room of the peoples
abusing the peoples.

The peoples studied singing themselves!—they know better,
they had piano lessons and have perfect pitch!

*The sacred art in fatal declining.*
*Give us back Ponselle, Melchior, Flagstad!*

*No wonder the poor cow had to steady herself on the rail,*
*apparently a sore throat, downed a glass of castor oil LOL*

*Rysanek couldn't find the right pitch with a GPS*
*Is this Aida a hyena?*

*Poor Renée—she tries, twice, to hit the high E,*
*and fails, twice.*

Poor Katia, poor Natalie, poor José, Franco.
Poor Monsterfat Cowbelly.

Poor Roberto, booed, shaking his fist, leaving the stage—
*plain unprofessional in my book dont be a sensitive bitch—*

understudy thrust forward—
*a nobody tenor in street clothes that looks like Big Foot.*

Poor Luciano, live *Spirito gentile* in '74—fine, really,
better than fine, a whole culture, a century, of legato,

except, yes, that one strangled C—
                                        and a captured chuckle

from some guy near the mike.

You, reader, listener, maker. If you think intention
is everything, go ahead,

try to make something good. Try to forget
that happy laugh.

## Long muteness at 46:12

Then after hiding Callas opened her eyes
and raised in profile
her pointy chin, one of her mad scenes,

but where's her voice?
I'm just a baby in a mud house in a mountain town,
so I can't help much. Maybe

Mom will take me to the opera,
pull on her black Dior with the plunging back,
ask me to sponge Max Factor over her scars.

Those little white moons.
At 44:06 her face had one hope, at 44:16 it flowed out
through her eyes. But where's her voice?

Her perfume was *My Sin*, her '50s console full
of opera from Dick Aspinwall, sometime afternoon guy
who asked did I want a knuckle sandwich. I know now

that when I'm nine I'll sing soprano,
Act One altar boy in *Tosca*, Trouble in *Butterfly*,
Marie's kid at the end of *Wozzeck* on his stick horse,

*hop-hop! hop-hop!* and I'll shake Stravinsky's hand.
I can't help this either,
but Dad might have worried less

about queers in the theater and more
about the afternoons he was away.
At 46:12 I'm still three so I won't hear it

for another 55 years, when finally
*—is it day or night, am I alive or buried—*
she opens her mouth.

# Callas vs. Jesus

Jesus includes Callas,
but Callas has no Jesus in her.

It being very Greek of her to ignore Him
in favor of His mother, and to count upon

her understanding of why a woman
would feel the need to say, over the radio,

"I would not kill my enemies,
but I will make them get down

on their knees. I will, I can, I must."

## "Goodbye, little table" at 02:15

While we two were together,
we only ever needed
one glass to drink from,

she sang.

## Rumors that Callas had a baby named Omero Lengrini

The earth, the dirt, it doesn't refuse
any step we might make today?

Not more than yesterday?
The space between atoms

isn't more remote, lonely, angry?

Because some of these mornings
when my foot first touches the ground

I have to cry
*mother     mother*

## Callas as Medea

Never type in the comments section
that "she had the voice of an angel."

Please, fool! What angel ever cried
*wronged, wronged, wronged* from all six tits

while warming her feet at a fire
made with the other soprano's pretty hair?

One feather of the firebird, it's said,
could light a darkened room.

If you must type something, type "a voice
of white phosphorous, of ichor,

of the Centralia mine fire still burning after fifty-four years,
of a cloak made with flayed angel skins

with their caroling tongues still attached."
Because what you see when with her nightshade

Callas X-rays the dark room where you thought
you were alone,

is the feathered gods at work,
bringing death to the living

and raising the dead to life.

## Tombeau: At the grave of Maria Callas

*—an empty niche in the Columbarium Père-Lachaise, Paris*

She whom you seek is not here!
Don't put your ear to the earth;
she is not in the earth.

Begotten by Apollo
upon Litsa Dimitriadou,
famous for a downward chromatic plunge

and terrible mistakes in love, finally her myth
was scattered over the Aegean.
So if anything

put your ear to the sea. Its menses
hoisted up by the moon,
then let fall

when that fucking rock turned
its jealous, songless face
away.

# Callas and the First Noble Truth

You critics threw her ashes into the sea
Complaining "She had three discrete voices."
But how good did you think you deserved things to be?

All life is unsatisfactory,
Buddhism teaches.
You critics threw her ashes into the sea

Just as other critics shot good Jack Kennedy
And left him in pieces.
But how good did you think you deserved things to be?

Saying "Let God deliver her, if He
Delight in her noises,"
You critics threw her ashes into the sea,

Sinatra too, Garland, Elvis, Coltrane, Stravinsky,
Now nothing but traces.
But how good did you think you deserved things to be?

Dead in Paris at fifty-three,
No Greek to retrieve her from Hades,
You critics threw her stolen ashes into the sea.
But just how good did you think you deserved things to be?

## Envoi: Callas and my mother say goodbye

I.

After whoever filched her urn
From its niche in the columbarium

Then—sleepy? bored?—set it down
(I'm making up this part now) on

Christmas Day on the Path of the Dragon,
It was Vasso decided on the Aegean.

The sea being the one place
Where when you put something,
You always know where it is.

A windy day, her ashes
Blew back in their faces,

Their mouths.

II.

Following me,
Watching, listening,
Writing this, you can't save me.

Out the window I'll sleepwalk
Again over the rickety
Mill race.

I'll wake up
(It's in my music)
Again on the divan of some man

Not your father. And again
I'll cross the Alps
On just

My exhaled breath

## Bruna's hand

You went to her niche in '87, stole a white rose
Bruna her maid had left.

Bruna's hand left a rose and your hand
carried it away.

# The primal uses of Callas

After about a million births, the soul recognizes the scent
of placenta carried from a darkened room in a bowl,

destined for a variety of ancient uses.

## I Heard the Voice of Jesus Say

*Allahu akbar*, a moment

of no one injuring anyone anywhere.

It was after his bath and the evening

was cool and crickets.

He hummed the tune to "Lilac Wine,"

*(I feel unready for my love...)*—

then whispered—*God . . . is . . . extreme . . .* —but didn't

mean me, I think, or anyone

to overhear.

# I told Jesus When I was afraid

as a child, I looked for pictures of you in the encyclopedia and circled them around my bed.

Jesus said, I remember Giotto, Cimabue, Fra Angelico. I remember the bells as Duccio's *Maestà* was carried into the cathedral.

I told Jesus, I asked you to lift my gayness from me, laid down on my face in front of the altar at All Saint's Church on West Fort Street in Detroit. I was nineteen, it was 1975, midnight and the tiles were cold.

Jesus said, I remember asking you Hath the rain a father? or who hath begotten the drops of dew?

I told Jesus, for thirty years I asked you to send me someone to love, and then Stephen came and we married, but we were old, so I begged you, keep us alive, let us live a little longer.

Jesus said, I remember I remember I remember the poem of you
that I sent to the empress with a branch of flowering.

, Giulietta
/2, and
static
at Fateh
the
e robes
a which
sand-
f
le in
Kuya
ny
uth,
fingers
ar 700,

# apiosexual Confession: On Patrick Do
## wn Operas (Four Way Books 2019) Toward Pe

y, sometimes smothering, almost shaming
t air, which swore
s night how
r in the middle of your heart."

—from "Honey"

e, Special to VOICE

Donnelly is quoting
Don Giovanni in that
ely his own translation,
ed devotion. I confess
rills me, awakens,
own Operas says
art—You've been
small, you need larger
age I read only what
to write the instant the
es yet these poems also
ne a better person before
out. Poetry affirms a soul of infinite grasp beyond
net Patrick twice and emanating waves of his
tle, stirred the room each moment.

Patrick Donnelly

**f Christ Carrying the Cross,**

vanni Bellini circa 1505 oil on wood, is what
en his third and fourth weekly pill boxes,

mself to reorder. His routine about the anti-
eater magnitude, maybe, than the one in which

er used to place a vase of violets in front
ing, when she owned it. This card's only

tion of the Passion, not the original. But we've seen
on and daily use can make of pity and fear

cozy utensil. The Savior's torso is pointed
royal climb, but his unreadable eye turns out,

you, passerby, a tear of blood and milk.

oets such as Anne Carson, David Ferry, Jane Hirshfield,
lly braid contrasting narratives and materials into
blooms of unsurpassed, sublime tone—he's gathering
gy of such poems which clued me in. Renowned
nsky writes—"Here is a Gospel According to Patrick
a book of revelations of what it means to be human, to
be awed, to be stunned by our world—and to find love

late in life. It is a book of tender
in pain, everyone who's been ill,
loved music, everyone who's live
sun. What should one do when
voices so present, so generous, s
full of bewilderment and hilarity
take this book and do what Mrs.
in this book) would do: place a v

Tennessee Williams was onc
doing, anyway?" So lovely, so wo
you know, writing about love, ho
rocks."

**Maria Callas went to Hambur**

In 1959 when Maria Callas we
was still neoclassical. In the film
7 seconds, silk legs the clappe

But the moment I need to tell
of the Pirata aria, when resting
on the conductor's cage, head
thirty seconds forty fifty, she doesn't k
descending figure, strings distresse

(remember Mom in the '60's? her c

Shameless wooing brought fo
statement from Patrick—"My lin
valley behind many pillars of fire,
Whitman, Allen Ginsberg, Chris
Walter Jackson Bate's biography o
*River-Merchant's Wife: A Letter,* W
Tennyson's inconsolable In Mem
Judy Garland (dead at 47), Fred A
*One For My Baby,* Lorraine Hunt
*Steps,* then dying at age 52, Moza
friends' tears already flow over o
cantata *Ich Habe Genug,* Nina Si
delusional in *Lilac Wine,* Beetho
sung by Fritz Wunderlich (dead f
likely drunk, his shoes badly tied,
LaMontagne singing *Trouble,* Iris
*Cry, The Tale of Heike, The Tale of*
John Dowland's *Flow My Tears* an
the *Policeman Said,* all of Diane S

# onnelly's rfection of Tone

ess toward everyone who's been
everyone who's had a mother,
d on this third planet from the
one encounters a book of
questioning, physical, so
, so kind? I, for one, want to
Gardener (one of the people
ase of violets in front of it."
e asked, "What are you
rld- weary, he replied, "Oh,
w violets break through the

g

nt to Hamburg her hair
n she emerges at 0 minutes:
r of an underwater bell.
about is at 42:30, prelude
her left hand
d down eyes closed, cloistered,
how us, we are nowhere and no one,
ed, dissonant, trembling, swelling,
oor closed, sometimes till noon—)

rth this priceless, bookable
eage: I walk this lonesome
not all of whom are poets: Walt
opher Smart, John Keats and
f Keats (dead at 25), Pound's *The*
Villiam Meredith's *The Illiterate*,
oriam, Maria Callas (dead at 53),
staire, Frank Sinatra singing,
Lieberson singing, *As With Rosy*
t's song *Abendemfindung* (our
r grave; he died at 35), Bach's
one, drunk, abandoned and
en's *To the Far-Away Beloved*
om falling down the stairs,
at 35), Rufus Wainwright, Ray
DeMent singing *No Time To*
*Genji*, and *The Pillow Book*,
d Philip K. Dick's *Flow My Tears*,
ess's poems, Pedro Almodóvar's

*Talk to Her* and *Bad Educatio*
Masina, Fellini's *La Strada*, *8*
*La Dolce Vita*, the howling, ec
qawwali songs of the late Nusr
Ali Khan, the Hebrew psalms,
black church baptizing in whit
in a river in Melbourne, Florid
I saw when I was six, the thous
and-one golden bodhisattvas o
mercy at Sanjūsangen-dō temp
Kyoto, the statue of the monk
at Rokuharamitsu-ji with six ti
Buddhas coming out of his mo
and the incomparably delicate
of Miroku Bosatsu, from the ye
in the treasure house of Kōryū-ji."

**Rumors that Callas had a baby named Omero Lengrini**

The earth, the dirt, it doesn't refuse
any step we might make today?

Not more than yesterday?
The space between atoms

isn't more remote, lonely, angry?

Because some of these mornings
when my foot first touches the ground

I have to cry

*mother mother*

Poet, editor, professor, Patrick Donnelly and his spouse, Stephen D. Miller, also translated classical Japanese poems in *Th Wind from Vulture Peak: the Buddhification of Japanese Waka in the Heian Period* (2012). Find his Wikipedia entry, and YouTube of interviews and readings.

---

**Richard Jarrette**—author of *Beso the Donkey* (2010), *A Hundred Million Years of Nectar Dances* (2015), *The Beatitudes of Ekaterina* (2017), *The Pond* (2019), editor with Red Pine *Dreaming of Fallen Blossoms: The Tune Poems of Su Dong Po*, Yun Wang Translator (White Pine 2019), *Toward a Hidden River With No Human Name: A Memoir, Poems* (March 2020).

Notes & Acknowledgments

For a U.S.-Japan Creative Artists Fellowship that funded three months in Japan during 2014, during which I wrote some of these poems, I'm grateful to the Japan-U.S. Friendship Commission, the NEA, the Japanese Agency for Cultural Affairs (*Bunkachō*), and the International House of Japan. Special thanks to Christopher Blasdel, Sawako Nakayasu, and Manami Maeda in Japan, and Paige Cottingham-Streater and Margaret Mihori in the United States, for support and friendship before, during, and after my time in Japan.

For time at the Vermont Studio Center as a visiting writer in 2015, thank you to Ryan Walsh and Laurie Macfee.

For long support of my writing and teaching, thank you to Michael Collier and Jennifer Grotz of the Bread Loaf Writers Conference.

To my companions on the path, Adrian Blevins, Laurel Blossom, Vievee Francis, Kathleen Graber, Jennifer Grotz, Michael Klein, James Allen Hall, Henry Israeli, Joan Larkin, Diane Seuss, and Tania Rochelle, thank you for advice on these poems.

For supporting my work and life, deep thanks to James Arthur, Justin Bigos, Clifford Browder, Christina Davis, Carl Dennis, Maudelle Driskell, Jane Hirshfield, Tony Hoagland, Ilya Kaminsky, Susan Kan, Mary Ruefle, Dinah Stevenson, Daniel Tobin, Chase Twichell, Spencer Reece, Laurel Rasplica Rodd, Ellen Doré Watson, Larry Schourup and Isao Sano.

Deep gratitude to Martha Rhodes, Ryan Murphy, Sally Ball, Bridget Bell, and Clarissa Long of Four Way Books.

For help corresponding in French with the Centre National du Costume de Scène about the cover image for this book, thank you to Rhonda Tarr, Senior Lecturer of French at the University of Massachusetts Amherst, Department of French and Francophone Studies.

To Stephen Miller, my first reader: "Oh know, sweet love, I always write of you, / And you and love are still my argument . . . "

The title *Little-Known Operas* is from a line of Albert Goldbarth's poem "Library"—"Shit: I forgot to send in the card, and now the Book Club has billed me *twice* for *Synopses of 400 Little-Known Operas"*—which, as 2015 - 2017 poet laureate of Northampton, Massachusetts, I produced as a short film: www.youtube.com/watch?v=EWyGPNWSka8

The "Jesus said" sequence that alternates with the other poems of this book was inspired by similar poems by Jean Valentine, from *Little Boat* (Wesleyan University Press, 2007), and also by "I Heard the Voice of Jesus Say," a hymn text by Horatius Bonar, 1846, arranged by Ralph Vaughan Williams using the Irish tune "Star of the County Down." Valentine's Jesus and mine have a family resemblance, but mine seems to be a gardener, a Sufi, an esoteric Buddhist, an atheist, a Japanophile, a sufferer of ocular migraines, and a fan of Federico García Lorca and Maria Callas.

The reader will notice that when Jesus introduces the topic of Maria Callas (as one does), a separate Callas sequence branches off from the Jesus sequence, and then, absurdly, recombines and argues with it. Hovering behind these Callas poems is my appreciation of a quote by Renata Scotto, recorded in conversation with Albert Innaurato:

> Listen to me, everyone speak about Callas. But I know Callas. I know Callas before she was Callas. She was fat and she had this *vociaccia*—you know what a *vociaccia* is? You go kill a cat and record its scream. She had this bad skin. And she had this rich husband. We laugh at her, you know that? And then, I sat in on a rehearsal with Maestro Serafin. You know, it was *Parsifal* and I was supposed to see if I do one of the flowers. I didn't. And she sing that music. In Italian of course. And he tell her this and he tell her that and little by little this voice had all the nature in it—the forest and the magic castle and hatred that is love. And little by little she not fat with bad skin and rich-husband-asleep-in-the-corner; she witch who burn you by standing there. Maestro Serafin he say to me afterwards, you know now something about *Parsifal.* I say, 'No, Maestro, I know much more. I know how to study. And I know that we are more than voices. We are spirit, we are god when we sing, if we mean it.' Oh yes, they will go on about Tebaldi this and Freni that. Beautiful, beautiful voices, amazing. They work hard. They sincere. They suffer. They more talented than Maria, sure. But

she was the genius. Genius come from *genio*—spirit. And
that make her more than all of us. So I learn from that.
Don't let them take from you because you are something
they don't expect. Work and fight and work and give, and
maybe once in a while you are good.

Which makes me, I guess, the muddy Colorado: "Carved with the curious legend of my youth" is from "Open the Gates" by Stanley Kunitz.

The chicken: after "The Illiterate" by William Meredith.

Honey: the Italian epigraph, translated in the poem's last line, is from Mozart's *Don Giovanni*, libretto by Lorenzo Da Ponte.

Jesus said Will someone: Sokaku's poem about the deer, co-translated by Stephen D. Miller and me, is 1956/1957 of the *Shinkokinshū*, the eighth Japanese imperial poetry anthology (1205).

Jesus said A program: "seven-storey bardos" is a shout-out to Thomas Merton's autobiography *The Seven Storey Mountain*, the title of which is itself a reference to Dante's Purgatory.

Throne Verse: the Throne Verse (*Āyat-ul-Kursī*) is the 255th verse of Surah Al-Baqara, the second chapter of the Qur'an.

Standing and moving: "There is no God but God," *la ilaha illallah* in Arabic, is the first half of the Shahada, the Muslim profession of faith;

the Rukeyser poem is "Islands." The poem is dedicated to the dead of the Pulse nightclub in Orlando, Florida, June 12, 2016.

Five objections to the practice of hammering nails into the heels of a corpse: this practice is among those described in Silvia Alfayé's "Sit tibi terra gravis: magical-religious practices against restless dead in the Ancient World" unizar.academia.edu/SilviaAlfayé/Papers/1254010/Sit_tibi_terra_gravis_magical-religious_practices_against_restless_dead_in_the_Ancient_World Two lines of Ezra Pound's "The River-Merchant's Wife: A Letter" are quoted in the poem.

Jesus asked: the passage in italics is from "A Major Work" by William Meredith.

Some temples: the italicized lines, beginning *Her salt tears fell from her,* are from Desdemona's "Willow Song," Act 4, scene 3 of Shakespeare's *Othello.*

One day one flower: the Frost quote is from "Directive," the Fellini film is *Juliet of the Spirits*; the Nō play is *Yoroboshi.*

In which I explain why I set the fire: the poem's Right and Left divisions are based on those of the Japanese imperial court in Heian-kyō (Kyoto) a millennium ago.

Jesus said Don't: In Buddhist eschatology, Maitreya is the Buddha of the future, the world teacher to come.

The moon: East Asian folklore identifies the markings on the Moon as a rabbit.

The ninth day of Av: Tisha B'Av is a day of fasting in Judaism, on which five calamities that took place in Jewish history are remembered, including the destruction of the First and Second Temples.

Lorca's lips: "maricón" is one of the many words in Spanish for "faggot" (every one of which, it seemed, I was called growing up in New Mexico in the 1960s).

Jesus said Just when I think: the Callas recording the poem describes is "Printemps qui Commence" from "Samson et Dalila" by Camille Saint-Saëns, 1961, Orchestre National De La Radioffusion Francais, Georges Prêtre conducting.

Maria Callas went to Hamburg: "Oh! s'io potessi dissipare le nubi" is the final scene from Bellini's *Il Pirata*; the minutes/seconds timing refers to the film of Maria Callas in concert, May 15, 1959. *Maria Callas In Concert: Hamburg 1959 & 1962*. EU: Warner Classics, 1999. DVD.

Crackup at 14:36: Callas had problems in the scena "Nel di della vittoria," from Act 1, scene 5 of Verdi's *Macbeth*; refer to the same film as "Maria Callas went to Hamburg."

Long muteness at 46:12: again the final scene from *Il Pirata*; same film as "Maria Callas went to Hamburg."

Callas vs. Jesus: the Callas quote is from a 1968 interview with John Ardoin.

"Goodbye, little table" at 02:15: Callas sang "Adieu notre petite table" from Massenet's *Manon*, in Paris, June 1963, with Georges Prêtre conducting. As in previous poems, the minutes/seconds in the title refers to a film of the performance. *The eternal Maria Callas.* EU: EMI Classics, 2007. DVD.

Envoi: I: After an unidentified person stole Callas's ashes from their niche in the Columbarium Père-Lachaise (abandoning them elsewhere in the cemetery), they were eventually recovered, then scattered over the Agean. II: Callas was a famous Amina, the sleepwalker of Bellini's *La Sonambula.* Though the opera ends happily, there's no guarantee that Amina's reconciliation with Elvino won't be disturbed if she sleepwalks again, away from his jealous supervision.

Bruna's hand: In the same 1968 interview with John Ardoin cited above, Callas spoke about Bruna Lupoli, her maid from 1954 until her death in 1977: "But when you can't trust your husband or your mother, to whom do you turn? When I go back to Paris, you know who takes care of me and who I know will always be there? My maid Bruna, who adores me and who has been a nurse, sister, and mother to me. She is only two years older. When I was in the hospital she didn't want the nurse to touch me, for she was ashamed to humiliate me, to have a nurse clean me. Imagine that such a person should exist today, and that's my kind of person. They are very rare. But she shouldn't have been there. It should have been my mother and my sister."

I Heard the Voice of Jesus Say: Takbīr is the term for the Arabic phrase *Allahu akbar*, sometimes translated "God is Great."

I'm grateful to the editors of the following journals and anthologies in which these poems previously appeared:

*American Poetry Review, Bellevue Literary Review, The Cimarron Review, Guesthouse, Kyoto Journal, Mudlark, Salmagundi, Tikkun, Plume, Waxwing.*

*Academy of American Poets:* "Postcard of *Christ Carrying the Cross,*" Poem of the Day, March 16, 2015.

*Kenyon Review Online:* "Maria Callas Went to Hamburg," "Crackup at 14:36," "YouTube: Broadcast Yourself," "Long Muteness at 46:12," and "Envoi: Callas and my mother say goodbye."

All fifteen of the Jesus poems were included in *Jesus Said*, a chapbook from Orison Books, July 2017.

*The Plume Anthology of Poetry*: "Tombeau: At the grave of Maria Callas," 2018; "Throne Verse," 2013.

Cover Art: Costume designed by Franco Zeffirelli and created by Marcel Escoffier for Maria Callas in the Paris Opera's 1964 production of Vincenzo Bellini's *Norma.* Used with permission of the Centre National du Costume de Scène, Moulins, France. CNCS © Pascal François

PATRICK DONNELLY is the author of four books of poetry. Former poet laureate of Northampton, Massachusetts, Donnelly is director of the Poetry Seminar at The Frost Place, and an associate editor of *Poetry International.* His poems have appeared in *American Poetry Review, Slate, Ploughshares, The Yale Review, The Virginia Quarterly Review, Hayden's Ferry Review, The Massachusetts Review*, and many other journals. Donnelly's translations with Stephen D. Miller of classical Japanese poetry were awarded the 2015-2016 Japan-U.S. Friendship Commission Prize for the Translation of Japanese Literature. Donnelly's other awards include a U.S./Japan Creative Artists Program Award, an Artist Fellowship from the Massachusetts Cultural Council, the Margaret Bridgman Fellowship in Poetry from the Bread Loaf Writers' Conference, and an Amy Clampitt Residency Award.

Author photo: Carl Nardiello

Publication of this book was made possible by grants and donations. We are also grateful to those individuals who participated in our 2018 Build a Book Program. They are:

Anonymous (11), Sally Ball, Vincent Bell, Jan Bender-Zanoni, Kristina Bicher, Laurel Blossom, Adam Bohanon, Betsy Bonner, Mary Brancaccio, Lee Briccetti, Jane Martha Brox, Carla & Steven Carlson, Caroline Carlson, Stephanie Chang, Tina Chang, Liza Charlesworth, Andrea Cohen, Machi Davis, Marjorie Deninger, Patrick Donnelly, Charles Douthat, Emily Flitter, Lukas Fauset, Monica Ferrell, Jennifer Franklin, Helen Fremont & Donna Thagard, Robert Fuentes & Martha Webster, Ryan George, Panio Gianopoulos, Chuck Gillett, Lauri Grossman, Julia Guez, Naomi Guttman & Jonathan Mead, Steven Haas, Lori Hauser, Mary & John Heilner, Ricardo Hernandez, Deming Holleran, Nathaniel Hutner, Janet Jackson, Rebecca Kaiser Gibson, David Lee, Jen Levitt, Howard Levy, Owen Lewis, Sara London & Dean Albarelli, David Long, Katie Longofono, Cynthia Lowen, Ralph & Mary Ann Lowen, Jacquelyn Malone, Fred Marchant, Donna Masini, Catherine McArthur, Nathan McClain, Richard McCormick, Victoria McCoy, Britt Melewski, Kamilah Moon, Beth Morris, Rebecca Okrent, Gregory Pardlo, Veronica Patterson, Jill Pearlman, Marcia & Chris Pelletiere, Maya Pindyck, Megan Pinto, Taylor Pitts, Eileen Pollack, Barbara Preminger, Kevin Prufer, Vinode Ramgopal, Martha Rhodes, Peter & Jill Schireson, Jason Schneiderman, Jane Scovel, Andrew Seligsohn & Martina Anderson, Soraya Shalforoosh, James Snyder & Krista Fragos, Ann St. Claire, Alice St. Claire-Long, Dorothy Tapper Goldman, Robin Taylor, Marjorie & Lew Tesser, Boris Thomas, Judith Thurman, Susan Walton, Calvin Wei,Bill Wenthe, Allison Benis White, Elizabeth Whittlesey, Rachel Wolff, Hao Wu, Anton Yakovlev, and Leah Zander.